Activity
Manual for
Adolescents

For bulk purchases at reduced prices of Activity Manual for Adolescents, please contact the Sage Special Sales Department nearest you.

SAGE Publications, Inc.
2455 Teller Road
Thousand Oaks, California 91320
E-mail: order@sagepub.com

SAGE Publications Ltd.
6 Bonhill Street
London EC2A 4PU
United Kingdom

SAGE Publications India Pvt. Ltd.
M-32 Market
Greater Kailash I
New Delhi 110 048 India

Activity Manual for Adolescents

Cheryl L. Karp
Traci L. Butler
Sage C. Bergstrom

IVPS

SAGE Publications
International Educational and Professional Publisher
Thousand Oaks London New Delhi

For information:

 SAGE Publications, Inc.
2455 Teller Road
Thousand Oaks, California 91320
E-mail: order@sagepub.com

SAGE Publications Ltd.
6 Bonhill Street
London EC2A 4PU
United Kingdom

SAGE Publications India Pvt. Ltd.
M-32 Market
Greater Kailash I
New Delhi 110 048 India

Printed in the United States of America

0-7619-0949-4 paperback

98 99 00 01 02 03 10 9 8 7 6 5 4 3 2 1

Acquiring Editor: C. Terry Hendrix
Editorial Assistant: Dale Mary Grenfell
Production Editor: Michele Lingre
Production Assistant: Denise Santoyo
Typesetter/Designer: Andrea D. Swanson

Contents

93770

PHASE II: EXPLORATION OF TRAUMA

PHASE III: REPAIRING THE SENSE OF SELF

PHASE IV: BECOMING FUTURE ORIENTED

1 | *Adolescent Social and Sexual Development*

❑ Teen Talk

In order for you to understand and appreciate just how much your history of abuse has affected you as an adolescent, we thought it might be helpful to take a look at some of the issues that come up during adolescence, including normal adolescent social and sexual development. As you grow from infancy to adulthood, you move through specific developmental periods. What happens during this process has a critical effect on how you function later on. Therefore, if you were abused as a young child, that will have an effect on how you handle things as a teenager and as an adult. Although gay and lesbian issues are relevant to normal sexual development, we felt that they deserved a section of their own. Therefore, this topic is covered in the section following "Overview of Normal Sexual Development."

Although we realize that emotionally and physically abused teens often suffer as much as sexually abused teens, the following sections refer more to sexually abused teens. Because sexual abuse may have a major impact on later sexual and social development, we felt it was important to single this area out for discussion.

OVERVIEW OF NORMAL SEXUAL DEVELOPMENT

Many sexually abused teens have questioned what "normal" sexual development is. Therefore, we have included a review of normal sexual development as well as abnormal sexual development. Hopefully, this will cover issues that you feel are important to address in your treatment.

Sexual development occurs in progressive stages. In regards to sexual ability, from birth children have occasional erections or vaginal secretions, and by the age of five any child is capable of experiencing sexual feelings. In addition, cultural norms come into play when evaluating what is *normal vs. abnormal* sexual development. What may be normal for one culture may not be regarded as normal in another culture. For example, some cultures feel it is normal to date at ten while another culture may feel this is too early to begin dating.

The term "latency-age" refers to children from 7-12 years of age. Children in this stage engage in a range of sexual interests. They continue to have peer contact in school, they may also begin to experiment with sexual behaviors, and they may have alternating periods of being sexually "open" and sexually "secret." Children in this age group vary a great deal. This period of development was first labeled "latent" because it was thought that this was a quiet stage of development, but it appears that this was a mistake as this period is far from a dormant or inactive stage of development.

According to many experts in the field of development, from the age of nine or 10, most boys engage in a rich form of experimentation that is best characterized as "silent sex"—they sit and fantasize for hours about the differences between males and females. Children of this general age group may appear less interested in sexual topics due to what they have learned as adult rules about sexual matters and have, therefore, become more secretive and private about their sexual thoughts, feelings, and behavior.

Developmentally, preadolescents (10-12 years) are focused on establishing relationships with peers. Many preadolescents, and certainly adolescents (13-18 years), engage in sexual activity with peers, including open-mouth kissing and sexual fondling, and some adolescents begin to have intercourse. Adolescents and some preadolescents find themselves *falling in love*.

Children are likely to take on the culture's values about sex and nudity even if their families' values are different. The culture's moral, religious, and health restrictions on sexuality may cause some adolescents to engage only in forms of sexual activity that do not involve sexual intercourse (such as oral sex) and may cause others to fear and/or avoid all sexual contact until much later.

Masturbation begins as in early childhood with a small percentage of children, but by 13 years of age, 80% of children are engaging in masturbation. There is also an increase in sexual play with other children the same age, from about 5% at 5 years of age to about 65% at 13 years of age. In spite of strong societal feelings against the practice of masturbation, it soon becomes the primary sexual activity for most adolescents. During adolescence, there is also a marked increase in sexual activity and interest in both sexes.

Adolescence is often described as a time of transition into adulthood. This can be a trying time, for you are no longer viewed as a child, but you are not yet truly regarded as an adult. This can cause internal conflict as you strive to separate from your parents and become your own person. In addition, the beginning of adolescence signals the onset of puberty for some teens, which results in rapid changes in sexual development. Puberty can actually begin as early as 10 years of age or as late as 16 years of age.

The changes in sexual development brought on by puberty can be a source of concern, anxiety, and preoccupation for many teens. The timing, how fast the changes are happening, and the types of physical changes experienced may have different effects, especially on girls' self-image and self-esteem. Society's obsession with the "perfect" body has resulted in the quest for "thinness" as reflecting "beauty." For boys, the physical changes seem mostly to raise self-esteem, probably because of society's positive attitude toward masculine characteristics.

Sexual development in adolescence involves more than just physical changes or behavioral changes related to puberty. According to many experts, sexual development also involves developing a healthy sense of your sexuality. This includes

1. Learning about intimacy through interaction with your peers
2. Developing an understanding of personal roles and relationships, both within and outside the family
3. Revising or adapting your perception of your body to changes in physical size, shape, and capabilities, especially during your early adolescence
4. Adjusting to having erotic feelings and experiences and integrating them into your life
5. Learning about what standards and practices society expects regarding sexual expression
6. Developing an understanding and appreciation of the reproductive process

Puberty is generally thought of as the time when the body becomes capable of reproducing. For girls, puberty begins when they first get their period. This normally occurs between the ages of 10 and 16 years. *Secondary sex characteristics,* such as breasts and pubic hair, also begin to appear at this time.

For boys, the signs of puberty are more subtle. They include the development of facial, pubic, and other body hair, as well as the lowering of the voice due to the lengthening of the vocal cords. This is also when most males experience a growth spurt, including an increase in height, weight, musculature, and physical strength.

Other signs of sexual maturity for the male during adolescence may include "wet dreams," the beginning of masturbation to ejaculation, and an increased interest in the opposite sex. Sometimes male adolescents are described as "raging hormone machines" or "hormones on wheels" to emphasize the sudden increase in hormones at puberty.

GAY AND LESBIAN ISSUES

Gay and lesbian issues often emerge during the teenage years. Although most sexual experiences in adolescence are heterosexual, it is common for preadolescents and adolescents to have some same-gender sexual feelings and experiences. During this stage of development, many teens begin to suspect that they are gay, lesbian, or bisexual.

Many specialists in human sexuality take the view that very few adults are exclusively hetero- or homosexual, no matter how they choose to label themselves. These researchers feel that most people fall somewhere in between.

We believe in taking a nonjudgmental stance toward the issue of sexual orientation. Sexual orientation is an important part of an individual's personality. However, stereotypes, ignorance, and misinformation still create an environment in which discrimination can thrive. Fear of rejection by peers and parents has placed many gay, lesbian, and bisexual adolescents at risk not only for low self-esteem but also for suicidal thoughts and behaviors.

Some teenage girls and boys are reluctant to disclose any sexual abuse by someone of the same sex because they fear that peers and adults will think they have become gay as a result. Their own fears of same-sex intimate relationships may also cause intense shame and guilt. Also, many girls who have been abused by men mistakenly believe the myth that such experiences make women become lesbian.

At the present time, no one clearly knows why heterosexuals are heterosexual and homosexuals are homosexual, although there are many theories. Research suggests a strong genetic biologic connection to homosexuality. Twin and other family member studies suggest a possible genetic link within the family. We believe that rather than focusing on the origin of sexual orientation, your focus should be on common abuse experiences regardless of orientation.

DIFFERENCES IN MALE AND FEMALE VICTIMS

Because there are lots of differences between the experiences of boys and girls who have been the victims of sexual abuse, we have decided to cover some of the differences with you. These differences concern both the abusive experience itself and how you understand and make sense of the experience.

If you are a teenage boy who has been sexually abused, cultural beliefs and stereotypes of femininity and masculinity may make you see yourself as less than male, as a "woman," (i.e., powerless) or as homosexual. These interpretations are not useful when working on your trauma issues. These kinds of beliefs may even add to the pain and confusion that you have already experienced as a result of being abused. Therefore, it is important to assess whether you hold any of the beliefs or stereotypes about yourself. If you do, you need to discuss this with your therapist.

Another belief that you may have is that no matter what, all sexual activity is good for males. When a sexually mature female victimizes a boy, this may be seen as "scoring" by his peers. Films portraying sexual abuse of males by females in a romantic light or as an initiation into the grown-up world of sexuality are a powerful reinforcement of this belief for a young man.

You may not want to accept that the female abuser's behavior gratified her needs rather than yours. But even if you do not consciously view this experience negatively, it still affects you negatively and can influence your subsequent behavior and relationships. On the other hand, if you are a teenage girl, you are much more likely to see your victimization as harmful and as an affront to your personhood.

The belief that male victims automatically become sexual abusers may prevent some of you from disclosing your abuse. This belief can add to the guilt and shame of your abuse. If you have also acted out sexually, you may feel safer discussing the acting-out behavior than discussing how you have been abused yourself. This is because society makes it difficult for males to describe themselves as vulnerable. Therefore, many abused boys do not look for support from their peers, nor do they seek out counseling.

One thing that female and male victims have in common is that they are both more likely to be abused by males. Boys are more likely than girls to be victimized by someone outside the family. For example, adult authority figures outside the home, such as babysitters, coaches, teachers, scout leaders, and family "friends," are more likely to abuse males than family members are. In addition, boys are much more likely to be physically abused along with the sexual abuse.

For some of you, this may be the first time you have ever discussed your abuse with other peers in a group setting. This is important, since many male and female teens have felt alone in having been abused. Often they have kept it secret from others and felt isolated. We encourage you to talk with peers from your group, both in group and outside group. They can be a nice support group for you.

You will experience lots of feelings as you go through the recovery process. Boys may have to learn how to deal with anger constructively before moving into emotions such as shame, guilt, and grief. Girls may first need to work on their tendency to get stuck in depression or to hurt themselves. Underneath the depression is often lots of rage or anger that needs to be dealt with also.

Activities found in Chapter 3 of this book ("Feelings")—for example, "Feelings Charade"—can help you discover a range of emotions. Developing assertiveness skills will help you to manage your anger. Reading stories and watching videos that deal with childhood abuse, violence in dating relationships, communication skills, and issues related to cultural norms and stereotypes may serve as nonthreatening ways for you to share about your abusive experiences. Drawing and writing about your abusive experiences will also help you to work through the various emotions you feel.

ABNORMAL AND ABUSIVE SEXUAL BEHAVIOR

Many abused teens wonder if their behavior is normal or abnormal. Therefore, we decided to include this section to explain what behaviors are normal and what behaviors are not normal for children and teenagers.

For young school-age children (5-7 years), abnormal sexual behavior includes sexual penetration, genital kissing or oral sex, and "pretend" intercourse (humping behavior). For preteens and teens, abnormal sexual behavior includes sexual play with younger children (usually 4 or more years younger), as well as sex with someone your own age if you use force or threats to get it, if you manipulate the other person into it, or if you physically hurt the other person.

If you are wondering whether an experience you had was normal or abusive, we suggest that you ask yourself the following questions:

- Was one person controlling the other person?
- Was force or intimidation (scaring the other person) used?

- Did one person physically hurt the other in any way during the sexual experience?
- Was secrecy involved?

On the basis of what you read above, how age-appropriate were the sexual acts?

When you go for therapy, it is very important for you to understand that your relationship with the therapist will not be sexual in any way. If you are in a residential treatment center (RTC), you should also be aware that any adult working for the facility will maintain a supportive relationship with you but that, again, this will be nonsexual. You should be provided with information on the facility's grievance procedure, as well as on how to contact the local Child Protective Services office.

If there is information here that you don't understand, it is important to discuss it with your therapist. We hope that you now have a better understanding of your social and sexual development as a teenager. There are lots of resources available that can help in further understanding of what you have gone through. However, many of those books are written more on an adult level. You should ask your therapist for suggestions if you want to read more about abuse. We also encourage you to learn more about the consequences of unsafe sex, such as sexually transmitted diseases (STDs) and AIDS. Again, your therapist should be a good source of referral for you.

PHASE I

Establishing
Therapeutic Rapport

2

Who Am I?
Image Building,
Goal Setting,
and Therapeutic Trust

❑ Teen Talk

Teens who are using these activities have been emotionally, physically, or sexually abused. You, like the other teens who are working through this book, will be learning about yourself and your feelings. You will be able to understand better how your abuse makes you feel today and to learn healthier ways of taking care of yourself.

People who have been hurt use many different ways of trying to take care of their feelings. Sometimes they push their feelings down so that they don't have to feel them, or they claim not to have any feelings. Some people hurt others because they are hurting, and others hurt themselves in such ways as binging (overeating) and/or purging (throwing up), abusing alcohol or other drugs, or cutting on themselves. These are unhealthy methods of coping with stressful situations. This is why it is so important to learn to identify and express your feelings to safe people. How do you take care of *your* feelings?

The first step in taking care of your feelings is to share more about you and your family and to begin setting goals. The activities in this chapter provide many opportunities for you to do this so that you can begin your journey of becoming a healthier person. Good luck!

❑ **Activity #1: My Biography**

Name _____

Age _____ Date of birth _____

Hair color _____ Height _____ Weight _____

Grade _____ Name of school _____

My favorite teacher is _____

I live with _____

_____

Mother's name _____ Father's name _____

Where I was born _____

Favorite early childhood toy _____

I have _____ brothers and _____ sisters

Their names (and ages) are:

_____

_____

_____

_____

I am / am not happy with my family. (Circle one)

Things I like to do:

_____

_____

_____

_____

_____

Other things that I think are important to know about me are:

_____

_____

_____

_____

_____

My pets and their names: _____

_____

_____

_____

My best friend is: _____

❑ **Activity #2: Self-Portrait**

- Draw a picture of yourself that is as complete as possible.

❑ **Activity #3: My Family**

• Draw a picture of your family.

❑ **Activity #4: Family Activity**

- Draw a picture of your family doing something together.

❑ **Activity #5: My Three Wishes**

- What are your three wishes?

1. _____

_____

_____

_____

_____

2. _____

_____

_____

_____

_____

3. _____

_____

_____

_____

_____

❏ **Activity #6: Reflections of Myself**

- Look in a mirror, and write about or draw a picture of what you see.

❏ Activity #7: Self-Collage

- Look through different magazines, newspapers, and/or pictures for pictures, words, phrases, etc., that remind you of yourself. Arrange them on your paper however you want them. Glue them down.

❏ **Activity #8: I Like Me Because . . .**

- Write down 5 things you like about yourself.

1. _____

   _____

   _____

2. _____

   _____

   _____

3. _____

   _____

   _____

4. _____

   _____

   _____

5. _____

   _____

   _____

❑ **Activity #9: My Goals**

- Write down 5 things you would like to accomplish in working on yourself.

1. _____

_____

_____

2. _____

_____

_____

3. _____

_____

_____

4. _____

_____

_____

5. _____

_____

_____

3 Feelings

❏ Teen Talk

Everyone has feelings. A lot of times people will call feelings either "good" or "bad," but a feeling is really just a feeling. All feelings are okay. Your feelings may come from different experiences. What you see, hear, touch, smell, and taste may bring back thoughts and feelings from your past experiences.

Sometimes people who have been abused learn to "stuff" or put away their feelings so they don't have to feel them. The problem with stuffing your feelings is that it makes it hard to tell someone else how you feel and to identify your feelings about things that happened to you.

This chapter is to help you learn how to define and explore your feelings so that you can let others know how you feel. This may be a difficult task. It may make you feel vulnerable and unsafe. When some people feel unsafe they may begin to act out their feelings in unsafe ways.

You will also learn how to communicate your feelings to others so that other people will be able to understand just how you feel. This may feel uncomfortable and strange to you at first, but with practice it will get easier. The following activities will help you in your journey. Good luck!

❑ Activity #10: How Would You Feel?

- Write about what feelings you would have if you were in the following situations.

1. Your best friend wants to come over and spend the night with you.

_____

_____

_____

2. Judith worked very hard on her midterm paper, but she only got a D.

_____

_____

_____

3. Robert woke up in the middle of the night because he heard a strange noise.

_____

_____

_____

4. Ricardo was chosen to be the lead in the school play, but he had to drop out when his father couldn't drive him to rehearsals at night.

_____

_____

_____

❏ **Activity #11: My Feelings**

- Share your feelings by completing the following "I feel" statements.

1. I feel happy when _____

   _____

   _____

2. I feel sad when _____

   _____

   _____

3. I feel frustrated when _____

   _____

   _____

4. I feel scared when _____

   _____

   _____

5. I feel angry when _____

   _____

   _____

6. I feel proud when _____

   _____

   _____

7. I feel content when _____

_____

_____

8. I feel comforted when _____

_____

_____

9. I feel jealous when _____

_____

_____

10. I feel excited when _____

_____

_____

11. I feel worried when _____

_____

_____

12. I feel tired when _____

_____

_____

13. I feel silly when _____

_____

_____

14. I feel puzzled when _____

_____

_____

15. I feel insecure when _____

_____

_____

16. I feel brave when _____

_____

_____

17. I feel curious when _____

_____

_____

18. I feel rejected when _____

_____

_____

19. I feel trusting when _____

_____

_____

20. I feel strong when _____

_____

_____

❏ **Activity #12: Feelings Charade**

- This activity is designed to help you learn to express yourself and increase your ability to "read" other people's nonverbal body language. You can practice this activity with another person. You will need the list of 20 feelings listed below. You also need a set of 3-by-5 cards with a feeling written on each card. The feelings are divided according to the difficulty in expressing the feeling (#1 to #6 are considered easiest, #7 to #14 are considered medium, and #15-#20 are considered the most difficult). One person gets the list, and the other person gets the first set of feelings to act out nonverbally. The person with the list guesses what feeling the other is portraying. Move on to the next set and so on. Then switch places. This can be fun and challenging.

- Group 1: Happy, Sad, Frustrated, Scared, Angry, Proud
- Group 2: Tired, Worried, Silly, Excited, Jealous, Strong, Content
- Group 3: Insecure, Rejected, Trusting, Curious, Brave, Puzzled, Comforted

❑ **Activity #13: Feelings Collage**

- This collage is different from the one in the last chapter because it focuses on your feelings. Before you begin, sit quietly for a moment to clear your mind. Think about the feelings you want to portray in your collage. These can be feelings you have right now or feelings you had in the past. Cut out words, phrases, pictures, etc., that reflect these feelings. Arrange them on your paper and glue them down.

❏ **Activity #14: Feelings Mask**

- This activity is designed to help you look at any differences between how you feel on the inside and how you act on the outside.
- Take two paper plates. On one, draw how you feel most of the time on the "inside," and on the other, draw how others see you on the "outside."
- Then either staple or glue the backs of the plates together. Be sure to place the stick between the plates before putting them together.
- In the space below, you can write down what you think and feel about this activity.

❑ **Activity #15: Scrapbook of Feelings**

- This activity is designed to help you organize important feelings you may have felt in regard to different experiences in your life.
- Your scrapbook can be organized by feelings, time, or events.
- Buy a scrapbook or make your own.
- Begin collecting various items, magazine pictures, phrases, photographs, etc., that have meaning and/or represent feelings you have experienced.
- Once you decide how to organize your book, begin putting the items on the pages in your book.
- This is a project that may take some time to complete. Be as creative as you desire!

❏ **Activity #16: Feelings Essay**

- Look through the feelings listed in Activity #11, and choose a feeling to write about. Write about a time you felt that way. You can also include a picture if you desire.

_____

_____

_____

_____

_____

_____

_____

_____

_____

_____

_____

_____

_____

_____

4

Boundaries

❑ Teen Talk

When you were born, like everyone else, you had a special need to be protected and kept safe. Everyone has their own personal space and distance around their body which makes them feel safe. This is called your "boundary." When you were little, did you ever color a picture in a coloring book or have you played a game, like basketball, where you must stay within the lines? These are other examples of boundaries.

When someone is hit, touched in private ways, or yelled at, his or her boundaries have not been respected. Sometimes people think they are not being respectful only when they have hurt your body, but when they say hurtful things or when they don't take care of your basic needs such as providing clothes, medical care, food and shelter, they are still "violating" you and being neglectful.

If someone has hurt you in some way, this probably means you get confused about what is okay or not okay for people to do. It is important to learn how to keep yourself safe and how to be in control of your actions. This will also allow you to know when others are treating you with respect.

This chapter will help you learn what safe boundaries are, how to keep yourself safe, and how to be safe with others.

❏ **Activity #17: Developing Boundaries—Stop!"**

• After doing the activity described to you, read the following questions and answer them in the space provided. You may choose to share the answers or not.

1. What was it like to walk toward your partner not knowing when he/she would "Stop!" you?

_____

_____

_____

_____

2. Did you want to get closer or stay further away? What was that like?

_____

_____

_____

_____

3. What was it like to have someone walk toward you? Did you say "Stop!" sooner or later than you really wanted to? How did you know when to say "Stop!"?

_____

_____

_____

_____

4. If you had had a different partner (no names, please), might you have said "Stop!" at a different moment (closer or further away)?

_____

_____

_____

_____

5. What was it like to have your partner obey (or not) your "Stop!"?

_____

_____

_____

_____

6. Have you ever wished you could have said "Stop!" to someone in real life? When was this?

_____

_____

_____

_____

❑ **Activity #18: My Personal Space**

- Draw a picture of yourself, and color in the amount of "personal space" you desire to feel generally safe.

❑ **Activity #19: Sean's Story**

- Read the story and answer the questions.

Sean was having a difficult time. He lived at home with his father and older sister. Sean's father always seemed angry, especially when he was drinking. He would yell and hit Sean for no apparent reason. Now Sean was having problems with his own anger. This included getting in other people's faces when he was angry. He would also yell and push his friends at school. He started hanging out with gang members and started sneaking beer from the refrigerator.

Sean's teacher in one of his classes was helping him to understand what personal boundaries were and how to respect other people's "personal and private space." His teacher would tell him, "When your family has problems with respecting your personal and private space, it is hard to know how to respect others."

At home, everybody just did what they wanted without asking. Sometimes Sean's older sister would just walk in his room to get something without knocking or asking for permission to come in. Sometimes Sean was dressing.

Sean was now learning how to express his feelings with words. His teacher was also helping him learn how to ask permission before he "borrowed" his friends' things. This all seemed quite confusing to Sean, but he liked the idea of others respecting him and his belongings. Now he was hoping his family would learn about respecting his "personal space."

QUESTIONS

1. How did Sean's father and sister violate his boundaries?

_____

_____

_____

_____

2. How did Sean learn to be more respectful with his friends?

_____

_____

_____

_____

3. What do you think "personal and private space" means?

_____

_____

_____

_____

4. Draw a picture of Sean as you think he looks.

❑ **Activity #20: Identifying Healthy and Unhealthy Boundaries**

- The following is a list of behaviors that show what we are calling "healthy" or "unhealthy" boundaries. After having done the work in this chapter, you probably have a good idea of which one is which. There may be a few that you're not sure of; that's okay. Boundaries, just like many other things in life, are not always so clear-cut. That is why we need to learn and practice recognizing what our inner sense or "gut" feeling tells us.
- Read the list and decide which behaviors show healthy boundaries, which ones show unhealthy boundaries, and which ones could show either. Write "healthy," "unhealthy," or "either" in the spaces provided.
- Then choose one example from each of the three categories that you know about from experience: something that you did, or that someone else did to you, or that you saw someone else do to someone else. For each example, write a short description of the incident.

1. Telling your whole life history: _____
2. Having sex after a month of going together: _____
3. Asking for what you want: _____
4. Relating at an intimate level on the first meeting (using your own definition of *intimacy:* _____
5. Telling an acquaintance during your second week at your new school that you've had drug problems in the past: _____
6. Knocking on closed doors: _____
7. Falling in love with anyone who pays attention to you: _____

   _____
8. Asserting yourself when you want to stop sexual advances: ___

   _____
9. Being sexual when you first feel like it: _____
10. Asking someone if it's okay to give them a hug: _____
11. Going against what you believe in to please others: _____
12. Accepting money or gifts for sex: _____
13. Breaking up when someone is hurtful: _____
14. Giving as much of yourself as you can give for the sake of pleasing someone or maintaining your self-image: _____
15. Telling others no: _____
16. Having sex because the other person wants to: _____

17. Not saying anything when other people make you uncomfortable:
    _____

18. Being your own person even if it means not fitting in: _____

- Example of a healthy boundary:

    _____

    _____

    _____

    _____

    _____

    _____

- Example of an unhealthy boundary:

    _____

    _____

    _____

    _____

    _____

    _____

- Example of a questionable boundary:

    _____

    _____

    _____

    _____

    _____

    _____

❏ **Activity # 21: Boundaries and Personal Space**

- Write a definition and essay on what *boundaries* and *personal space* mean to you.

_____

_____

_____

_____

_____

_____

_____

_____

_____

_____

_____

_____

_____

PHASE II

Exploration
of Trauma

5 Developing Trust and Being Safe

❑ Teen Talk

Everybody deserves to feel safe and protected. People who have been hurt have had their trust violated. It usually becomes hard to trust others when you haven't been kept safe and protected. Sometimes it is even hard to trust yourself when others have hurt you because you may believe it was your fault. You need to know that whatever happened to you WAS NOT YOUR FAULT, NOR WAS IT YOUR CHOICE! Although at times you may have felt part of the decision making, the power and control was really with the person who hurt you.

This chapter will help you learn what trust is, how to trust yourself, and which people deserve your trust. You will also learn and explore what being safe means to you. This may be a difficult or even frightening process. It is important to communicate any feelings that you experience while you are working on these activities. Remember, it takes courage to use your words, and the courage is within you. Good luck!

❑ **Activity #22: Sara's Story**

- Read the story and answer the questions.

Sara was 10 years old. She lived with her mother in an apartment with her 2-year-old brother, Cameron. Sara's mother used to like going to nightclubs with her friends on the weekends. She told Sara that it was her time to have fun because she worked hard during the week.

There wasn't enough money for babysitters, so her mother used to tell Sara to watch Cameron for her while she went out. Sometimes she would even give her a dollar. Sara's mother would feed Cameron before she left. Then she would ask Sara to give him his bottle and put him to bed at 8:00 p.m. and to go to bed herself by 9:00.

On the nights Sara was left alone with Cameron, she often got scared, especially if her mother came home drunk. Sometimes she heard funny noises, and sometimes her mom brought home strange men. They would be laughing and making strange noises in the bedroom that woke her up. Sara shared a room with Cameron. She would lie awake and listen, hoping everything was okay.

Sometimes Sara got up and checked to see if her mom was okay because she heard her crying. One time, Sara actually saw her mom being hit. This really upset her, and she tried to help her mom, but her mom got angry at her and told her to go away. Sometimes Sara got hit and sent back to bed.

Sara learned not to open her door. On those nights, she did not feel very safe. She wanted her mother to tell her that everything was okay.

QUESTIONS

1. What does *being safe* mean to Sara?

_____

_____

_____

_____

2. What does *being safe* mean to you?

_____

_____

_____

_____

3. Is Sara old enough to babysit Cameron? If not, why?

_____

_____

_____

_____

4. What advice do you have for Sara?

_____

_____

_____

_____

5. What advice do you have for Sara's mother?

_____

_____

_____

_____

6. Draw a picture of Sara in the story.

❏ **Activity #23: My Safest Place**

  • Write an essay about the place where you feel the safest. You can
    also include a picture if you want.

_____

_____

_____

_____

_____

_____

_____

_____

_____

_____

_____

_____

_____

_____

_____

_____

❏ **Activity #24: Unsafe Places**

- Write an essay about the place(s) in which you feel unsafe. You may also include a picture.

_____

_____

_____

_____

_____

_____

_____

_____

_____

_____

_____

_____

_____

_____

_____

_____

❑ **Activity #25: Brian's Story**

- Read the story and answer the questions.

Brian was now 13 years old. He just had his birthday and was glad he was getting older, but he still wasn't big enough. He was not nearly as big as his brother, Chad, who was 17 years old. Chad was really big and used his size to get Brian to do what he wanted him to do.

Brian hated it when Mom and Dad went out on the weekends or to a meeting at school during the week because Chad would be left "in charge." Chad could be really mean. He used to make Brian rake all the leaves in the backyard and clean the dog messes, even though it was Chad's job. If Brian refused or said he would tell Mom or Dad, Chad would hit him and threaten to hurt him really bad if he told.

One day, Brian decided to stand up to Chad. He was tired of always doing what Chad ordered him to do, so he said "no." Chad started beating Brian up. He kept hitting his head in the ground. Brian had a bloody nose, a large knot on his head, and bruises. When his parents got home, Chad said Brian had had a bike accident.

Brian was afraid to tell. Chad would always apologize to Brian, saying he was sorry and that he would never do it again, but Chad always broke his promise.

QUESTIONS

1. Could Brian trust Chad in the story? Why OR why not?

_____

_____

_____

_____

_____

2. What should Brian do?

_____

_____

_____

3. Should the parents have known Chad was hurting Brian? Why/why not?

_____

_____

_____

4. Is there anyone you can trust? Who/why?

_____

_____

_____

5. What does *trust* mean to you?

_____

_____

_____

6. Draw a picture of Brian and Chad.

❏ **Activity #26: People I Trust**

- List the people you trust, and state why you trust each one.

1. _____

_____

2. _____

_____

3. _____

_____

4. _____

_____

5. _____

_____

6. _____

_____

❏ **Activity #27: Broken Trust**

- Write an essay about a time (or times) that someone broke your trust.

_____

_____

_____

_____

_____

_____

_____

_____

_____

_____

_____

_____

_____

_____

_____

_____

❏ **Activity #28: Being Assertive!**

• Read the following vignettes. Decide if the person in the story had an "assertive," "passive," or "aggressive" solution to the problem. Write your decision in the blank provided. If your response was "passive" or "aggressive," think of an assertive way to deal with the problem. You may want to consider factors that influence characters' behavior in the story.

1. You come home from school, put your books on the kitchen counter, throw your jacket on the couch, and say a brief "Hello" to your mother. You immediately go to your room to call your best friend to complain about what happened during your last class. A boy you liked called you a "bitch." All of a sudden, your mother walks in your room without knocking and yells at you to get off the phone to do your homework. You yell back at your mother that she never leaves you alone and that you have to talk to your friend NOW!

_____

2. Last night your mother and her new boyfriend were yelling really loudly at each other while you were trying to go to sleep. You didn't sleep very well because you had a bad dream about your parents having a big fight, like they used to before they got divorced. In class this afternoon, you "space out" because you are so tired. Your teacher accuses you of never paying attention. You start to cry and run out of the room. _____

3. Early on a Saturday, your father reminded your older brother to get the laundry done before he went to his football game in the afternoon. Later, he was again reminded by your mother. Your brother said he had to get going and walked out the door. Your mother looked upset, then asked you to do the laundry. You felt angry, but you did it anyway, partly because of your mother being upset. It's late now, and your brother has finally come home. You tell him that you didn't like him just leaving like that without doing his job and that you don't like getting stuck with his work. At least he should ask you first. _____

4. You have gone over to your best friend's house to study for a big test. Your friend seems really down and has no interest in studying. You try to cheer him up, but it doesn't help. You know he gets bummed out a lot, but you've always been able to get him to feel

better. He tells you he has a big secret and that you have to swear you will never tell anybody. Of course, you agree not to. Then he says that he's been thinking about death a lot lately, especially since his parents got a divorce. You are shocked and tell him you think he's crazy. He doesn't argue with you as you expect and just begs you not to tell anyone he's thinking about killing himself. He asks you if you want his CD collection. You tell him no, you aren't going to take this seriously. After hanging out for a while longer, with no one saying anything, you decide to go home. You walk home, feeling worried and confused. You decide to break your promise and ask your older brother for advice. _____

5. You are a junior in high school. While on a babysitting job, you meet the younger brother of the parent you are working for. He is very cute and a college freshman. He invites you out, which is very exciting and flattering. Your girlfriends are impressed. He takes you out to a nice restaurant and you feel very grown up. Finally a mature guy, you think. After dinner, he invites you back to his dorm room, which he shares. You figure this is safe because there will be a lot of people around. Once you arrive, everything is very quiet because it's a holiday weekend and a lot of people, including his roommate, have gone home. You tell yourself everything is fine. The only furniture in the room to sit on besides a desk chair is the bed. You sit on the chair and he sits on the bed. He asks you very sweetly to come and sit by him and you do so. All of a sudden, his arms are around you, and he's pushing you down on the bed. You try to sit up, but can't. When you start yelling, he lets you go. You run out of the room and down to the lobby, where you are glad to see a couple of people hanging around. You call your parents from a pay phone to come pick you up. You stay with the other people until they arrive. _____

6. You are a sophomore in a new high school. You are in an honors math class; your teacher is supposed to be one of the best teachers in school and a tough grader, so you are slightly intimidated by him at first. However, he makes a lot of jokes, so you start to relax. Besides, he's really kind of good looking. You are working on an assignment when all of a sudden you feel a hand on your shoulder. You are startled and look around; it's your teacher looking down at your work. You don't understand why, but it made you feel kind of "funny" inside. You have no friends yet, so you don't have any one to confide in. You decide you're just being silly and you should forget about it. _____

❏ **Activity #29: Safety Rules**

• Read the following rules to keep yourself safe:

1. It is okay to say "no" to someone who wants to get in your personal space.
2. It is okay to express any feeling, as long as you do not hurt anyone or anything.
3. Keep a safe distance from strangers or people that make you feel uncomfortable.

• List 5 more ways to keep yourself safe:

1. _____

_____

2. _____

_____

3. _____

_____

4. _____

_____

5. _____

_____

6

Secrets

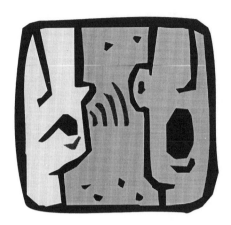

❏ Teen Talk

Secrets can be very confusing. There are times in our lives when it is important to be able to keep things "quiet"—such as a surprise party or a special gift. There are other times that you may want to keep something "confidential"—such as conversations you have with your therapist or conversations in group therapy. Also, there can be confusion between *privacy* and *secrecy*. *Privacy* may refer to times you keep your door closed (such as when you are dressing), whereas *secrecy* refers to intentionally concealing or hiding something.

There are times when keeping secrets can be harmful—for example, if the secret is about a friend wanting to hurt him- or herself, people doing something illegal, or people being hurtful to you. Difficult or "unsafe" secrets should not be kept quiet. These types of secrets can create all kinds of problems for you. They may make you feel worried, angry, sad, helpless, "dirty," and/or confused. It's okay to tell someone you trust about the things that make you feel uncomfortable inside.

Often, people who hurt kids tell them "not to tell." This may have happened to you. Sometimes they say that they will hurt you or your family or that something terrible will happen if you tell the secret. If this has happened to you, it can be very frightening to discuss what has happened.

It is important for you to know it is okay for you to share your past experiences with safe people. Sharing your difficult secrets is the best way of taking care of yourself. It is a way of validating that your experiences are important to you. Sharing these difficult secrets begins the process of letting go and allows you to move on.

This chapter will help you process the difference between "safe" and "unsafe" secrets. It will also assist you in exploring and deciding who you want to share your secrets with and when to do this. This can be a difficult hurdle to get over. Good luck!

❑ **Activity #30: Nikki's Story**

- Read the story and answer the questions.

Nikki was 13 years old. She wanted to go to summer camp like her friends. Instead, her mother told her that she was going to stay with her grandparents again. This made Nikki very upset. She didn't like going there any more. The summer had been a hard time for her mother ever since her mother and stepfather had gotten divorced. Her mother depended on Nikki's grandparents to watch Nikki and her younger sisters.

Nikki hated leaving the neighborhood, where she spent her time playing with her best friend, Karen, who lived in the same apartment building. She especially hated the "special" times when her grandfather would take her fishing. It was there that he had first touched her in her "private places." He told her that it was their "secret" and that no one would believe her if she told anyway. Nikki was confused. She used to like the special times they spent together, but she wished he would not touch her that way anymore.

As Nikki packed to go to her grandparents, she wondered if her grandfather had done anything like that to her mother. She wondered if she should tell her mother, but she really didn't want to burden her mother with her problems. She hated keeping this to herself, but she felt that her sisters were just too young to share this secret. Nikki also became worried because her next younger sister was just the age when grandpa had begun "touching" her. "If I tell, maybe we won't have to go visit there any more, but if I do, what will Mom do? She needs Grandma and Grandpa." Nikki was beginning to get sick as she thought about her secret.

QUESTIONS

1. What is the difference between safe and unsafe secrets?

_____

_____

_____

_____

2. What was Nikki's dilemma?

_____

_____

_____

_____

3. What was the *unsafe* or *difficult* secret in this story?

_____

_____

_____

_____

4. What do you think Nikki should do?

_____

_____

_____

_____

5. What would you do in a similar situation?

_____

_____

_____

_____

6. Draw a picture of Nikki.

❑ **Activity #31: Can We Talk?**

- Write an essay about who you can share your difficult secrets with. You may want to include why this is a safe person(s) and any experiences you may have had with sharing secrets.

_____

_____

_____

_____

_____

_____

_____

_____

_____

_____

_____

_____

_____

_____

❏ **Activity #32: My Friend's Secret**

- Write a story about a kid who was afraid to tell his/her difficult secret.

Once upon a time, _____

_____

_____

_____

_____

_____

_____

_____

_____

_____

_____

_____

_____

_____   THE END

_____

❑ **Activity #33: It's Confidential!**

- Write an essay about a time when someone told you something confidential.

_____

_____

_____

_____

_____

_____

_____

_____

_____

_____

_____

_____

_____

❏ **Activity #34: Secrets Make Me Feel . . .**

- Write an essay about how secrets make you feel. You can include examples of experiences you have had.

_____

_____

_____

_____

_____

_____

_____

_____

_____

_____

_____

_____

_____

_____

_____

7

Nightmares and Memories

❑ Teen Talk

Remembering everything that has happened is not easy. Remembering can be hard to do because it is sometimes painful to think about things you wish didn't happen. Sometimes, when things are too scary, you forget or "block" your memories, which might make you think nothing really happened.

Your dreams may be a way of helping you remember scary things. Scary dreams or nightmares are very frightening, but if you let them, they can help you. Exploring your dreams can help you learn more about things that have happened and about your feelings.

Many times, children see "monsters" in their scary dreams. This may have happened to you. It can be very frightening because the monsters seem so real, but as you know, there really are no monsters! Even as a teenager, you might continue to have frightening dreams.

Your dreams are pictures in your head, like a movie you may have seen. You can learn to have control over the frightening images, just as a director has control over a movie being made. The best way to control or direct your scary dreams is to share your thoughts and feelings about the dreams and about your memories of difficult experiences.

In this chapter, you will learn how to talk about the things you remember and your feelings. If you have scary dreams or nightmares, you will learn new ways to cope with them. Even though sharing frightening thoughts or feelings can be difficult, it is an important part of your healing process. We have included a fun activity that uses cartoon characters. As the song goes, "Free your mind and the rest will follow" (En Vogue).

❏ **Activity #35: I Had a Dream**

- Write about a dream you had.
- Then draw a picture of the most vivid part of the dream.

_____

_____

_____

_____

_____

_____

❏ **Activity #36: My Scary Dream**

- Write about and draw a picture of a dream that made you feel scared.

_____

_____

_____

_____

_____

_____

❏ **Activity #37: The Never-Ending Dream**

  • Write about and draw a picture of a dream that you have had more
    than one time.

_____

_____

_____

_____

_____

_____

_____

❑ **Activity #38: The Monster in My Dream**

- Some people see "monsters" in their dreams or other places. If you have had this experience, draw a picture of your "monster."

❑ **Activity #39: Cartoon Superhero**

- Draw a picture of a cartoon superhero that you think can help kids with their problems.

❑ **Activity #40: Superhero to the Rescue!**

- Draw a cartoon strip of your superhero helping a kid.

❑ **Activity #41: Significant Memories**

FIRST MEMORY

- Think back to a time when you were very young. Write about your
  first memory.

_____

_____

_____

_____

_____

_____

_____

_____

_____

_____

_____

_____

_____

BEST MEMORY

- Write about your best memory.

_____

_____

_____

_____

_____

_____

_____

_____

_____

_____

_____

_____

_____

_____

SADDEST MEMORY

- Write about your saddest memory.

_____

_____

_____

_____

_____

_____

_____

_____

_____

_____

_____

_____

_____

_____

_____

SCARIEST MEMORY

- Write about your scariest memory.

_____

_____

_____

_____

_____

_____

_____

_____

_____

_____

_____

_____

_____

_____

❑ **Activity #42: Memory Box**

- This activity is designed to help you make a special box to keep important reminders of difficult memories.
- The first step is to think about how you would like to decorate your box to keep your memories safe. Then decorate your box the way you want to.
- The second step is to collect things for your memory box. Choose anything that represents your difficult memories, such as pictures and objects.

PHASE III

Repairing the
Sense of Self

8 *Letting Go of Guilt and Shame*

❑ Teen Talk

Everybody wants to be cared for and be loved. The problem is that not everyone knows how to show his or her feelings in healthy ways. Sometimes others end up saying or doing hurtful things. It is very confusing when someone you are supposed to be able to trust hurts you instead of keeping you safe.

You may feel like it was your fault when others were hurting you. Their words and their actions may make you feel guilty and full of shame. It is not your fault when others make wrong choices and hurt you. The first thing you need to do is to talk about it and realize it was not your fault.

This can be a very sad time for you. You might feel like you have lost out on something because others have hurt you. You might even feel as if you have "lost" part of being a kid.

In this chapter, you will learn that other people's bad choices were not your fault. You will learn how to talk about your sadness and not feel so guilty. Hopefully, you will be able to learn how to let yourself have fun, not worry so much, and still be safe. Good luck!

❑ **Activity #43: Jared's Story**

- Read the following story, and answer the questions:

Jared sat in group. He was nervous. He had never really told his story before. He was sixteen now and in a residential treatment facility after running away. He had also spent time in the hospital for attempted suicide. No one knew just what was going on with Jared. He couldn't tell anyone. He was filled with tremendous guilt and shame.

Now he had been put in this group because he had admitted that he had been sexually abused on the intake form. He told his therapist that he was ready to tell his story, but was he? Now he was filled with doubts.

It had all started when he was 11 years old. He remembers how excited he was the day he finally got a "special friend." Jared lived alone with his mother and big sister. He had always wanted a big brother. His mother had filled out all the necessary papers so Jared could join a neighborhood club and become like a little brother to his "special friend."

When Jared met Ned, he found Ned to be warm and really nice. His mom also seemed to like him because he was so polite. The first few times, Ned took Jared miniature golfing. It was fun. They would then go out for hamburgers. Then, one day, Ned asked Jared if he would like to go swimming. It was a hot day, and Jared welcomed the idea. They went swimming at Ned's house. He had such a nice house and his own pool. Since it was now summer, they went swimming every week.

After about a month, Ned suggested they go "skinny-dipping." This felt strange, but since Ned seemed to think it was fun, Jared thought he would try it too. After all, Ned seemed so great. Everyone really liked him.

Skinny-dipping was kind of fun, but then Ned started leaving "adult" magazines on the bed whenever Jared went over. One day, Ned came in while Jared was drying off and started looking through the magazines. Then he did something that made Jared feel uncomfortable. He asked Jared if he had ever "played with himself." Jared didn't know what to say. Ned then told him he would show him how. He seemed to just want to help Jared, but it seemed strange. Ned assured Jared that it was a fun and normal thing to do.

This became part of the swimming outing every time Jared saw Ned. After a while, Jared was beginning to feel uncomfortable about going to Ned's. He didn't know what to say. He really liked Ned, but Ned began doing even more things with Jared that confused him.

Jared began to feel it was his fault for being willing to go skinny-dipping and look at the magazines with Ned. So one day, Jared just ran away. He went to stay at a friend's house. This became a pattern. Pretty soon, he stopped seeing Ned because he was always on restriction. This was a mixed blessing. He missed the time with Ned, but he didn't miss the "touching" and other sexual things. Jared wanted to just die!

QUESTIONS

1. Why did Jared think it was his fault?

   _____

   _____

   _____

2. What did Ned tell Jared that made him feel it was okay?

   _____

   _____

   _____

3. Why do you think Jared didn't tell his mother?

   _____

   _____

   _____

4. What do you think should happen to Ned?

   _____

   _____

   _____

5. What do you think you would do if you were Jared?

_____

_____

_____

6. When Jared's mom finds out what happened, what do you think she will do?

_____

_____

_____

7. Write about how you felt after reading the story.

_____

_____

_____

8. How can the group help Jared?

_____

_____

_____

❏ **Activity #44: My Story**

- This activity will involve writing about your own abusive experiences. You can then make your story into a book. First, you should write down a list of anyone who has hurt you. Then, write a page about each one. You can include a picture of each one. Then you should design a cover for your book. The book can be bound with paper fasteners, string, or cord.
- List the people who have hurt you that you want to include in your book.

1. _____

2. _____

3. _____

4. _____

5. _____

6. _____

7. _____

8. _____

9. _____

10. _____

❑ **Activity #45: I Would Say . . .**

- Reread your book, and write what you would like to say to each person who hurt you.

_____

_____

_____

_____

_____

_____

_____

_____

_____

_____

_____

_____

_____

_____

_____

_____

❑ **Activity #46: Thinking It Was My Fault**

- Complete the following sentences.

1. Sometimes I believe it was my fault because _____

   _____

   _____

   _____

2. Sometimes I believe it was my fault because _____

   _____

   _____

   _____

3. Sometimes I believe it was my fault because _____

   _____

   _____

   _____

4. Sometimes I believe it was my fault because _____

   _____

   _____

   _____

❑ **Activity #47: It Really Wasn't My Fault!**

- Read your last sentences, and rewrite them in the following sentences.

1. It was not my fault because _____

   _____

   _____

   _____

2. It was not my fault because _____

   _____

   _____

   _____

3. It was not my fault because _____

   _____

   _____

   _____

4. It was not my fault because _____

   _____

   _____

   _____

❏ **Activity #48: Me—Before and After**

1. Draw a picture of yourself before you were ever hurt.
2. Then draw a picture of your "hurt" self.

Before

After

❑ Activity #49: "Lost" Things

- When people have been hurt, they sometimes feel as if they lost something, such as their childhood.
- List the things you feel that you lost:

1. _____

   _____

2. _____

   _____

3. _____

   _____

4. _____

   _____

5. _____

   _____

6. _____

   _____

❏ **Activity #50: My Letter**

• Write a letter to your "hurt child."

Dear _____,

_____

_____

_____

_____

_____

_____

_____

_____

_____

_____

_____

_____

_____

_____

Love,

_____

_____

9 Working Through the "Stuck" Feelings

❑ Teen Talk

Congratulations! You have done a lot of good work dealing with your feelings. You've talked about difficult memories and experiences and how they made you feel. But you probably still have many other emotions. It is important to talk about these feelings as you begin to experience them. You may feel "stuck," but by having courage through sharing your thoughts and feelings, you can get yourself "unstuck."

You may start to experience anger at people who hurt you and didn't keep you safe. You also may be scared about letting your anger out. You can use your words, your artwork, and other skills you have learned to express yourself so that you don't lose control.

People who won't talk about their anger can become very sad, blame themselves, and even think about hurting themselves. Sometimes people hurt others because they are keeping their hurt, sad, and scared feelings locked up inside.

In this chapter, you will explore your anger and fear as well as grief or sadness related to your past experiences with abusive behavior. Hopefully, you will learn better ways to cope with your hurt, fear, anger, and grief. Please take this opportunity to deal with those difficult feelings. It is an important step in your recovery process. Good luck!

❑ **Activity #51: Sadness**

- Think about the things that are still causing sad feelings. Then list the things that still make you sad.
- Fill in the "I feel" statements for the things that still cause sadness:

1. I feel sad when _____

   _____

   _____

2. I feel sad when _____

   _____

   _____

3. I feel sad when _____

   _____

   _____

4. I feel sad when _____

   _____

   _____

❏ **Activity #52: Fear**

- Think about the things that are still causing scared feelings. Then list the things that still make you afraid.
- Fill in the "I feel" statements for the things that still cause fear:

1. I feel scared when _____

   _____

   _____

2. I feel scared when _____

   _____

   _____

3. I feel scared when _____

   _____

   _____

4. I feel scared when _____

   _____

   _____

❏ **Activity #53: Anger**

- Think about the things that still cause angry feelings. List the things that still cause you to be angry.
- Fill in the "I feel" statements for the things that still cause anger:

1. I feel angry when _____

_____

_____

2. I feel angry when _____

_____

_____

3. I feel angry when _____

_____

_____

4. I feel angry when _____

_____

_____

❑ **Activity #54: Tanya's Story**

- Read the following story and answer the questions.
- Then draw a picture of Tanya.

"Why did you do that?" Tanya was so angry that she didn't even notice that when she slammed the door, Randy was coming in the room and caught the door just before it slammed into him. Tanya had such a temper that whenever she was angry, she slammed doors or threw whatever was in her hand at the time. That had gotten her in trouble many times.

Tanya felt that no one understood her. She had been through so much. She was now living in a foster home. She was placed there after her teacher noticed the bruises on her arm and began questioning her about them. It wasn't the first time. Her mother had always told her that she deserved it, and she started thinking she did. After all, her father used to beat her mother, and her mother was always apologizing to him for doing something wrong. So Tanya started thinking it was her fault every time her mother hit her.

Now Tanya's counselor was teaching her how to gain control. She was working on a book about the different people who hurt her and how she felt about what they did. Now she was learning how to talk about her feelings. She also learned that taking a "time-out" sometimes helped her "cool down." Then she could talk about her feelings without throwing things or slamming doors. It was hard. Sometimes her anger just got the best of her—like today.

Tanya went to her room and opened up her journal and began writing. That was another good way to let out her feelings. She always felt so much better after writing. Then she was ready to talk about what was frustrating her.

QUESTIONS

1. What were the unhealthy ways Tanya took care of anger?

_____

_____

2. What did Tanya learn from her parents about anger?

_____

_____

3. Do you think this gives Tanya permission to act out her anger? Why or why not?

_____

_____

4. What were the healthy ways Tanya learned to take care of her anger?

_____

_____

5. How do you take care of your anger?

_____

_____

6. Are these healthy or unhealthy ways? Why or Why not?

_____

_____

7. What are healthy ways you can take care of your anger?

_____

_____

❏ **Activity #55: My Contract**

- Complete the following contract.

I will take care of my anger, hurt, and sadness by:

_____

_____

_____

_____

_____

_____

_____

_____

_____

_____

_____

_____

_____

_____

Signed by _____

❏ **Activity #56: Beginning My Journal**

• Write about your thoughts and feelings today.

Today I am feeling _____

_____

_____

_____

_____

_____

_____

_____

_____

_____

_____

_____

_____

_____

_____

_____

_____

❏ **Activity #57: You Hurt Me!**

- Write a letter to someone who hurt you. Make sure you tell how you felt about what that person did to hurt you.

To: _____,

_____

_____

_____

_____

_____

_____

_____

_____

_____

_____

_____

_____

Signed_____

_____

PHASE IV

Becoming
Future Oriented

10

What Have I Learned?

❏ Teen Talk

You've done a great job! You have learned how to identify and express your feelings in ways that are not hurtful to you or others. You know more about safe boundaries and how to protect your personal space. You have learned what trust is and what *being safe* means. You have learned the difference between safe and unsafe secrets.

You have worked on how to share your memories and the feelings that go along with them. You have learned that your dreams can sometimes help with your memories and are really your mind's eye looking at unresolved issues.

You have learned that you are not responsible for other people's bad choices when they hurt you and that in fact you really had no choice or responsibility for what happened. You also learned that now you have the choice to express your angry and hurt feelings in safe ways.

Wow, you really have learned a lot! But healing your hurt feelings takes time. You can't always make your hurt go away as fast as you may want. This chapter will help you decide how much you have learned and what you still need to address. Congratulations on a job well done!

❑ **Activity #58: Pride List**

- After all of the work you have done, you have a lot to be proud of.
- Write about the things that make you feel proud.

_____

_____

_____

_____

_____

_____

_____

_____

_____

_____

_____

_____

_____

_____

❏ Activity #59: Self-Affirmations

- List or write about the things you like about yourself.

_____

_____

_____

_____

_____

_____

_____

_____

_____

_____

_____

_____

_____

_____

_____

❏ **Activity #60: Things I've Learned**

   • Write about the things you have learned.

   _____

   _____

   _____

   _____

   _____

   _____

   _____

   _____

   _____

   _____

   _____

   _____

   _____

   _____

   _____

   _____

❏ **Activity #61: Self-Portrait**

- Draw a picture of who you are now.